ML ++
636.4 D157
Dalgleish, Sharon.
Pigs

WITHDRAWN

Farm Animals

Pigs

Sharon Dalgleish

CHELSEA CLUBHOUSE

An Imprint of Chelsea House Publishers
A Haights Cross Communications Company
Philadelphia

This edition first published in 2005 in the United States of America by Chelsea Clubhouse, a division of
Chelsea House Publishers and a subsidiary of Haights Cross Communications.

All rights reserved. No part of this publication may be reproduced or transmitted in any form or by any
means without the written permission of the publisher.

Chelsea House Publishers
2080 Cabot Boulevard West, Suite 201
Langhorne, PA 19047-1813

The Chelsea House world wide web address is www.chelseahouse.com

First published in 2005 by
MACMILLAN EDUCATION AUSTRALIA PTY LTD
627 Chapel Street, South Yarra, Australia, 3141

Associated companies and representatives throughout the world.

Visit our website at www.macmillan.com.au

Copyright © Sharon Dalgleish 2005
Copyright in photographs © individual photographers as credited

Library of Congress Cataloging-in-Publication Data

Dalgleish, Sharon.
    Pigs / Sharon Dalgleish.
    p. cm. -- (Farm animals)
    Includes index.
    ISBN 0-7910-8272-5
    1. Swine--Juvenile literature. I. Title.
    SF395.5.D375 2005
    636.4--dc22

                                                    2004016192

Edited by Ruth Jelley
Text and cover design by Christine Deering
Page layout by Domenic Lauricella
Photo research by Legend Images

Printed in China

Acknowledgments

The author and the publisher are grateful to the following for permission to reproduce copyright material:

Cover photograph: a family of pigs, courtesy of The DW Stock Picture Library.

Australian Picture Library/Corbis, pp. 5, 7, 20 (top and bottom), 21 (top), 24, 28; Corbis Digital Stock,
p. 14; The DW Stock Picture Library, pp. 1, 4, 6, 8 (top and bottom left), 10, 16, 21 (bottom), 26, 27;
Getty Images, p. 11; Getty Images/Photodisc, pp. 8 (bottom right), 9; Bill Thomas/Imagen, p. 25;
G. R. Roberts © Natural Sciences Image Library, pp. 8 (center), 29; © Peter E. Smith, Natural
Sciences Image Library, pp. 13, 15; Photodisc, pp. 3, 18; Photolibrary.com, pp. 17, 19 (top and bottom),
23; United States Department of Agriculture, pp. 22, 30.

While every care has been taken to trace and acknowledge copyright, the publisher tenders their
apologies for any accidental infringement where copyright has proved untraceable. Where the attempt
has been unsuccessful, the publisher welcomes information that would redress the situation.

FOND DU LAC PUBLIC LIBRARY

+
36.4
D157

Contents

What Is a Pig?

A pig is an animal with a large, flat nose called a snout. Pigs can be white, pink, black, spotted, red, and even blue. All pigs squeal and make an "oink" sound.

Pig tails are short and sometimes curly.

The adult female pig is called a sow. The adult male is called a boar. The young are called piglets. A group of pigs is called a herd.

Pigs often stay together as a herd.

Sows

Sows give birth to piglets. They have large **litters**. An average sow can have 6 to 13 piglets in one litter.

A sow will stand between her piglets and any danger.

Boars

Boars have strong necks. They also have a very large tooth sticking out each side of their mouth. These teeth are called tusks.

Some farmers trim the boar's tusks.

strong neck

trimmed tusk

Life Cycle

Piglets grow up to have piglets of their own, and the life cycle continues.

Piglets are born with their eyes closed. They can walk soon after they are born.

When they are three months old, piglets can do without their mother's milk. These young pigs are called **weaners**.

Adult boars and sows **mate** to produce piglets.

Piglets

The first thing new piglets do is scramble for the best spot to drink milk from their mother.

The first-born piglet gets the best spot near the sow's head.

Growing Up

When the piglets are a few days old, the sow takes them outside. At first, the piglets stay close to their mother. After about two weeks, they begin to explore.

After three weeks, the piglets begin to copy the sow.

The smallest piglet in the litter is called a runt. If there are too many piglets, the runt will miss out on milk. The farmer will try to find another sow to feed it, or bottle-feed it.

The runt is usually bottle-fed.

Farm Life

Pigs are noisy. They oink, squeal, and grunt throughout the day. They can make about 20 different sounds to talk to each other.

Sound	What It Means
short grunt	the pig is happy
long grunt	the pig is very happy
several quick short grunts	the pig is angry
20 grunts in a row	the pig is hungry
squeal	the pig is in pain

Pigs cannot sweat through their skin like people can. They keep cool by stretching out on a cool patch of earth. They can also roll in a muddy puddle.

Pigs also stand in water to keep cool.

13

Eating

Farm pigs eat a lot. But they are not greedy. They need plenty of food and water to stay healthy. The average farm pig spends a total of about two hours a day eating.

These pigs are eating breakfast slops from a trough.

Pigs dig in the ground for tasty roots, worms, or insects. This is called **rooting**. Pigs have a special digging tool—a snout!

Pigs have flat snouts and a good sense of smell.

Playing

Pigs play and explore. They are very smart. In fact, they are as smart as dogs.

Pigs explore their pens.

Sleeping

Pigs sleep for about 13 hours a day. The piglets sleep huddled together in a tight group.

Piglets sleep close together to keep warm.

Pig Farming

Some farmers keep pigs for their meat. Pork, ham, and bacon all come from pigs. Pig skins can be made into leather.

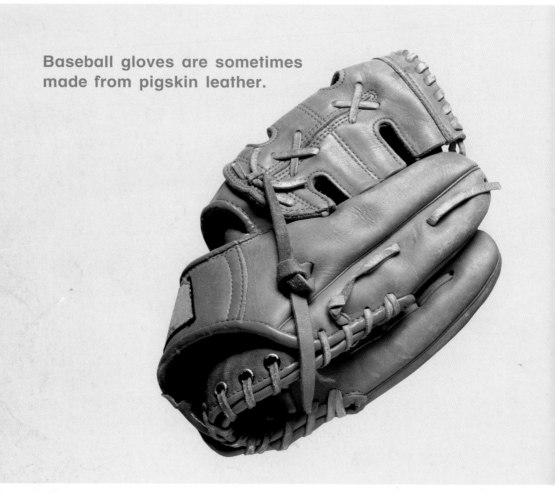

Baseball gloves are sometimes made from pigskin leather.

In France, pigs are kept to find truffles. A truffle is a type of **fungus** that grows underground. Truffles are tasty and very expensive.

Truffles grow in shady areas under trees.

Pigs can find something buried underground 20 feet away.

19

Pig Breeds

There are more than 500 pig **breeds** in the world. Pigs that are bred for bacon have a slimmer, longer body.

Yorkshire pigs are large white pigs. They can weigh more than 1,000 pounds and are bred for bacon.

Landrace pigs grow quickly, and are bred for bacon. They have large ears that flop over their eyes.

Pigs that are bred for pork have bigger muscles.

Gloucester Old Spot pigs have big hams, and produce a lot of pork.

Duroc pigs are red in color and are bred for pork. They usually need less feed than other pigs.

Looking After Pigs

Farmers look after pigs by building shelters. Sows need a warm place to make a nest for their piglets. The shelter is large enough for just one sow and her piglets.

A sow with piglets needs to have shelter in her pen.

Pigs are curious and like to wander. Farmers must check all the fences. A weaner can squeeze through a small hole in the fence. Bigger pigs can crash right through weak fences.

Fences must be strong so that the pigs can't get out.

Feeding

Pigs are easy to feed. They eat many different types of food such as corn, wheat, and oats. The farmer pours the food into troughs two to four times a day.

Pigs rush to the food trough when the farmer tips in the food.

A sow with new piglets stays under shelter with her piglets for the first few days. The farmer must give her food while she is busy looking after her piglets.

A sow stays inside to feed when she has new piglets.

25

Cleaning

Farmers clean the pens. Pigs are very clean and even piglets will try to keep the nest clean. Pigs will use the far corner of the pen as a toilet.

Pigs keep their pens fairly clean.

Watering

Pigs need to have their skin wet often, especially in hot weather. The farmer must make sure there is clean water for the pigs to bathe in, or damp earth to roll on.

Trees provide shade for pigs in large pens.

Moving Pigs

Moving a stubborn pig is not easy. To stop a pig, a farmer might hold something in front of it. Pigs don't see very well so it will think it is a wall.

Farmers sometimes move pigs with their hands.

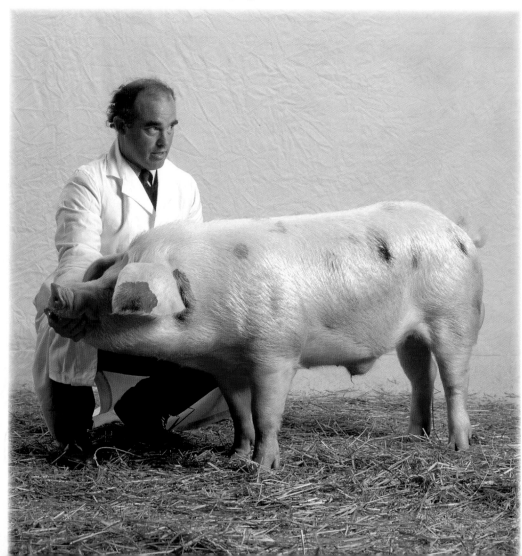

How to Call a Pig

What to do

1 Stand outside the fence so a pig doesn't sneak up behind you.

2 Call "piggy" as loudly as you can.

A pig will come to you when called.

Farm Facts

- A piglet weighs about 3 pounds at birth. It will double its weight in seven days.

- Pigs have four toes on each hoof. But they walk on only two of the toes on each hoof. They look like they are walking on tiptoe.

- Piglets drink about 32 glasses of milk a day.

- Another name for a farm pig is a hog. Some farmers only call a pig a hog when it weighs 120 pounds or more.

Glossary

breed   a group of animals that have the same set of features

fungus   a plant without leaves, such as a mushroom or a toadstool

litter   groups of piglets born at the same time to the same sow

mate   when a male and female join to create their young

rooting   digging with the snout

weaner   a young pig that no longer needs its mother's milk

Index